THE
DAY
HOLLY
TOOK ON THE
GOVERNMENT

THE DAY HOLLY

TOOK ON THE GOVERNMENT

HOLLY HAIL

To order additional copies of this book, contact:
Xlibris
UK TFN: 0800 0148620 (Toll Free inside the UK)
UK Local: 02036 956328 (+44 20 3695 6328 from outside the UK)
www.Xlibrispublishing.co.uk
Orders@Xlibrispublishing.co.uk
818618

To my grandson Gordon-Leigh.

CONTENTS

PREFACE

When my grandson is of age and able to read this book, he will know how much I love him and how I fought for his freedom to be with his mum. I am deeply saddened that my grandson never had the chance to know his great-grandmother like I have. If social services had allowed my mother to have seen her very first great-grandchild, then I am sure she would not have died, and my grandson, Gordon-Leigh, would have had many great memories of his great-grandmother. This book is the experiences I have encountered and is fact, not fiction.

I have had to change all names and places in this book because of confidentiality and legal reasons.

ACKNOWLEDGEMENTS

I would like to thank my daughter for having no objection to me writing this book. I would also like to thank my children for their patience and understanding when there have been times when they had to do with a Chinese or down the fish-and-chip shop. For on those occasions, I have been busy writing my book. (God bless them.)

I would also like to thank Dave Pelzer. By reading his books, he inspired me very much to write my own book about the experiences that I have had of the system. I have never met Mr Pelzer, but I feel that I can relate to him. We have both been victims of the system, although our circumstances are not the same, and the system still has failed us. The system in America failed Dave as they had many opportunities to realize that he was being abused by his mum long before he had to suffer the abuse that he did; whereas, the system in Britain should have realized that I was not an abuser, but the social workers who were in charge chose to take it personal with my Asperger's syndrome and used their powers way beyond necessity. These social workers very nearly destroyed my life and my family.

CHAPTER 1

THE LIVING NIGHTMARE

It all started on a day when my 15-year-old daughter Michelle went into the social services department and told them that I had *battered* her.

Two social workers from the child protection team from Taffcard came to my home and said, 'Hello, Mrs Gail. We are from the child protection team. Can we come into your house as we have concerns about an incident that your daughter Michelle and her boyfriend Wally told us about?'

I stood and looked at them for a long time, not knowing what to do.

It was only when my husband said 'You had better come in' that I realized I had been staring into space with disbelief.

It was the woman who introduced herself first as Mrs Lewis. She then said to me, 'This is my companion Mr Jones.'

I had noticed that Mrs Lewis took an instant dislike to me, and she had already judged me before I had even opened my mouth to speak.

Mr Jones sensed this because he was trying to be very nice to me, or was he trying to trick me into a false confession of abuse to my daughter?

I said to Mr Jones, 'There had been an incident but not what my daughter had portrayed it.' I explained that Michelle was very difficult, rude, and violent towards me, and I did go to smack her on the bottom as a form of chastisement.

Mrs Lewis then replied very sternly, 'Your daughter is pregnant, Mrs Gail. You should not be smacking your daughter whilst she is pregnant.'

I tried to explain that my daughter Michelle did not act as if she was pregnant. She acted like a ten-year-old spoilt child.

Mrs Lewis would not listen to whatever I had to say. I then looked at Mr Jones for sympathy as I felt that he was not judging me.

I said to Mr Jones, 'I did not realize that I could have harmed my daughter's baby by smacking her on the bottom. Not many 15-year-olds end up getting pregnant.'

Mrs Lewis informed me that social services would like to put my daughter into care and asked if I would be willing to sign forms for her to go into care.

At first, my husband said he had had a gutful of his daughter with her staying out at night and using abusive language to her mother, also being violent to her mother, as well as being violent to her brothers, and not taking responsibility for her pregnancy and putting her unborn baby at risk with her waster of a boyfriend Wally. She was not even willing to listen to good advice given to her concerning her. 'Give me the forms,' he said. 'I will sign them. It might do her some good. It might wake her up a bit and find out what the real world is like instead of being in a fantasy world. She is under the impression the grass is greener over the other side.'

My husband was just about to sign them when I snatched the forms out of his hands, saying, 'You're not signing those forms just because Michelle has caused a lot of problems. You do not give up on her. I am not going to let you sign those forms. We will always be there for our daughter, no matter what she goes through.' You don't have a puppy for Christmas and then have it put down.

Mrs Lewis tried all she could to persuade me to put my daughter into the care system by saying, 'Mrs Gail, we have experts who can help your daughter.'

'That is a laugh,' I replied. 'Where were the experts for my daughter when I went to your department desperately begging for help for her when she was taking drugs? I even went to the police department, given the police the drugs pusher's name and address, telling them that this person was supplying drugs to underage teenagers. I told the police officer I wanted him arrested and taken out of commission as he was a very dangerous man. Mr. Evans, chief superintendent at the time, told me to go away as I did not know what I was dealing with and leave it to the experts that know best. "You are just a distraught mother.

Go home and get a life with your family." This was why I went to your department to get help for my daughter and spoke with a duty social worker, Mrs Cassandra, but sadly, she turned me away too, telling me the same thing, that I was a distraught mother and to go home. I just wanted some advice on how to stop my daughter from taking the drugs, especially how to handle the comedown from the drugs.'

I told Mrs Lewis, 'My husband and I have never taken drugs other than prescribed drugs from our GP.'

At the time, there weren't any rehabilitation centers like there are today, and there certainly was not any literature telling you about drugs. Today they send the literature into the schools. Children can come home with literature telling them the effects drugs can have on them if they were to take it, but when my daughter took the drugs, there was no literature anywhere. I did not know who to turn to.

I asked my mum what I should I do. The advice she gave me was go to the police, which I did. However, that did not work. I asked my mum again, and she told me to go to the social services. As you know, I did. I had no help with my daughter. I got my daughter off the drugs by myself.

I asked Mrs Lewis why the department did not help my family when I went there for help.

Her reply was, 'I cannot answer that as I was not on the case at the time. You will have to take it up with the social worker you spoke to at that time.'

I said to her, 'How convenient. Tell me, are all social workers trained to say that?'

She made no comment on that. Then she said, 'I take it then, Mrs Gail, you are not prepared to put your daughter into care.'

My reply was, 'You got that in one, Mrs Lewis. How observant you are.'

Mr Jones informed us that our daughter Michelle was refusing to come home and that we should ring Warry social services to find out what was happening with my daughter. Mr Jones smiled and shook our hands and left. I chose not to shake the hand of Mrs Lewis.

Straight after they left, I rang the social services, asking where my daughter was. The only information I could get was from a receptionist, saying that Michelle was refusing to come home and that I was to ring again in the morning and speak to a social worker called Mrs Wiggins.

I told the receptionist that I was not going to leave my daughter at that office as I was afraid that social services would send her far away from her family so I would never see her again.

I said, 'I had been told many stories by mothers where social services had sent their children far away from their families and the parents never saw their children again. I am catching the next bus to this office to take my daughter home, where she belongs.

When I arrived at the social services department, requesting to see my daughter, the look on the social worker's face said it all. Mrs Wiggins was not happy to see me. The social worker told me to go home.

My reply to her was 'Not without my daughter. Please go and get her.'

The social worker asked the receptionist to show me to a room whilst she went and got my daughter. I was shown into a room opposite the reception desk. The room had five small chairs and several boxes of children's toys. Obviously, this was a room where mothers had to go when needed to be interviewed.

I was on my mobile phone, talking to my husband, when Wally walked into the room and strolled in behind my daughter that acts as if she didn't care about the world.

I said to my husband, 'I will ring you later, love,' and closed the mobile phone and put it down in front of me on the coffee table.

I then looked towards the door where the social worker was standing with a smug grin on her face. I pointed to my daughter's boyfriend and said, 'You better get him out of here before I do something I might regret later.'

Mrs Wiggins turned slightly with a huff, saying, 'Come on, Wally, let me show you where the kitchen is, and you can make yourself a cup of coffee.'

I said under my breath, 'Let me shuck the coffee over him.'

The social worker turned around and asked, 'What did you say?'

'Nothing,' was my reply, and they both went out of the room.

Michelle came and sat by the side of me with her head facing down, looking at the floor.

I lifted her face into my hands and looked at her and said, 'Why did you go to social services and tell them I battered you?'

She looked at me in the eyes, with tears that rolled down her cheeks. 'I never, Mum. It was Wally who said that you battered me.'

I let go of my daughter's face and burst out, crying. I said to her, 'You really don't know what you have done, do you?'

She said it was Wally's idea to go to social services. He had told Michelle because he had been in the care system, he knew how the system worked. He said to Michelle that if she tells social services that her mother battered her and made it believable, then she will be given a two-bedroom flat, and it will be furnished, and we can play happy families.

I then said to her, 'It doesn't work like that.'

Her reply was, 'What do you know? You're only my mother. Mothers don't know everything.'

'I don't pose to know everything, Michelle.'

She said, 'I am not coming home.'

'Why, for heaven's sake?' I said.

'I don't want to,' she said rather flippant.

Mrs Wiggins, the social worker, had entered the room just as Michelle told me she was not prepared to go home. The social worker had a massive grin on her face. I could tell she was pleased that my daughter was refusing to go home.

"As you see, Mrs Gail, your daughter is not prepared to go home. Perhaps you can sign for Michelle to stay at childminders for one night.'

I replied, 'How can I be sure that I won't be signing for my daughter to go into care?' I once signed a form from my solicitors, being told that it was a form preventing my ex-husband taking my son out of the country, when, in fact, it was a care and control order form for my son to be in my mother's care.'

'Oh, I can assure you it will not.'

'You can't assure me anything. I refuse to sign any forms.'

Holly thought to herself and wondered what became of Mr Biro Mail. She does believe he immigrated to New Zealand. *God help them in New Zealand.*

I said to Mrs Wiggins, 'If I cannot persuade my daughter to go home, then I have no alternative but to let her stay one night with the childminder. I am not happy about it and do not give permission for my daughter to go into the care system. I will be here first thing in the morning to pick her up, so have her ready.'

I then left, telling my daughter that I loved her and I will be there first thing in the morning to collect her.

On the bus going home, I was thinking to myself, will she be able to cope at the childminders?

I arrived home, and my husband asked, 'Where is Michelle?'

'She did not want to come home, and she is staying one night at childminders.'

All that night, I could not sleep, thinking and worrying about my little girl.

I took the bus in the morning to the social services department. I walked into the reception area and asked, 'Where is my daughter, and can you go and get her?'

My daughter was silent and refusing to speak.

I broke down, crying, telling her that I loved her and missed her. 'All I want is for you to come home, where you belong. Your brothers missed you very much, and they want you home. You know, I have done nothing wrong. Why you are punishing me like this?'

Michelle asked if she could talk to me alone before anything was decided.

The receptionist took us to the same room where we were the day before. I went to sit down, and even before I sat, she blurted out that she did not like it at the childminders and was made to feed and change a baby.

A friend of the childminder brought her baby to see the childminder, and Michelle was told it would be good practice for her when she gets her baby. But what they did not anticipate was it frightened Michelle to the extent of having nightmares. It was the wrong action to take to train my daughter to be a good mum because they forgot she was only a child herself.

She said, 'Please, Mum, I want to go home.'

I ran out of the room, shouting, 'My daughter wants to go home!'

I went looking for the social worker Mrs Wiggins. I found her talking with another mum. I told her that my daughter was going home with me.

The social worker informed me that she had to speak with her manager before I could take her home.

I said she could speak to the queen, for all I care, no one is preventing my daughter from going home.

I went back to the room where my daughter was, and after a very long wait, the social worker returned and said that there has to be a case conference.

'Why?' I asked.

'Just procedure,' she said.

'What procedure? Don't you mean you want to put my daughter on the risk register?'

'Just because there is a case conference does not mean that your daughter will be put on the risk register.'

'I don't believe you. You want to take my daughter away from her family and put her baby up for adoption.'

I was so angry with the social worker that I never gave her a chance to answer. I said, 'Come on, Michelle, let's get out of this awful place before I get arrested for doing something I will regret later.'

My daughter was just standing there, bewildered. I grabbed hold of her hand and gently walked her out of the building. We then went home, and I told my husband all that happened.

Michelle said to me that the social services were talking and she overheard them saying there was a place for her a hundred miles away. So what I had said to the social worker was true. If my daughter had not gone home with me when she had, I probably would not have seen her ever again.

THE NIGHTMARE CONTINUES

Eight weeks went by, and I heard nothing from the social services department. I thought that they had realized that my daughter was not quite telling the truth about the incident and that the social worker, Mrs Wiggins, believed that I had done nothing to my daughter. I thought social services were going to leave our family alone.

My daughter Michelle became more difficult, and she would not listen to any advice given to her. All I was trying to do was make her see the reason that she could not go gallivanting around Taffcard pregnant—she had to think of the baby. I tried to tell her that Wally was a known drug taker and he was no good for her, but she could not see any reason. I only had her best interests to heart.

I was speaking with a lady on the bus when I was going to town. I told her about the problems I was having with my daughter not listening to good advice from her mum and the fact she was pregnant at 15, so young.

I did warn the social services that my daughter will end up getting pregnant if she did not come home, but all the social worker said to me at the time was she will come home in her own time.

Yeah, she came home, all right, *pregnant. Why didn't anyone listen to me?*

I was telling the lady I did something stupid—I took in a young lad because he was homeless. He had just come out of prison, and he was a friend of a friend of my husband's. My husband knew that I would not be able to say no. My heart went out to him. I never thought for one second that my daughter would end up being his girlfriend. I thought that she would have more to attend to like her pregnancy. I did speak with my children about taking in Wally. They were not happy about it, but I had promised him I would take him in. At first, I said no because my children were not happy about it, but he came to my door with a cardboard box with all his belongings. He was like a lost puppy. I just couldn't say no.

At first, things were going great. I told the woman he was heeding to my rules. He was staying away from my daughter, and he was smoking outside, but then all things went pear-shaped. My daughter became his girlfriend, and he was back on the drugs, and I was not sure if my daughter was taking drugs. It did not seem that she was taking drugs because she was not behaving like when she was on the drugs before.

I said to the lady I really need to get this lad out of my house. He is a bad influence to my daughter and my children.

The woman said, 'Yes, dear, you need to get him out. I suggest you go to the social services department, being he is under 18.'

I really did not want to go there, but I had no choice but to get him out of my home.

The next day I went to the social services and asked to speak to a duty social worker. I could not believe my eyes when it was the same lady I saw when I tried to get help for my daughter when she was taking drugs, Mrs Cassandra. I thought I could ask why she did not help my daughter back then, but I thought better of it. I wondered if she was going to help this time.

I explained the situation, saying I needed to get Wally out of my house because he was not good for my family.

Her only comment was I should not have taken him in in the first place.

'You don't say . . .'

She then said it was not the social services' responsibility but the council's.

Guess what the council said? *Yeah, you got it.* Not their responsibility either.

However, I was told by the nice, kind gentleman from the council if I got no joy from social services, there were homeless hostels I could try. He gave me the phone number of the hostel, and I thanked him very much.

I never bothered to go back to the social services. I got a room in a homeless hostel for Wally. He was not pleased, but I did not care if he had to go. I had all the shit from my daughter telling me I was cruel to kick him out, but I knew I was doing the right thing.

Social services were back on the scene again because a probation officer from the Salvation Army where Wally was staying had concerns for my daughter hanging around places that were not suitable for a pregnant teenager. My daughter was not taking care of herself, and I was worried about her and her unborn baby, but what could I do? She would not listen to me.

I rang social services on numerous occasions and asked if I could speak with a social worker. I was always told that someone would get back to me, but no one ever did. It was at this time that social services took my daughter to a doctor to be examined. I was forbidden to go with my daughter. They said my daughter was old enough to decide for herself, and she did not want me there, even though my daughter was under 16 years of age and it was against the law to examine her without one of her parents being present. I told social services I did not want the examination to go ahead, but they still went ahead with it.

When my daughter came home, I asked her why she did not want me there at the examination. Her reply was she was never asked for me to be there. 'The social worker just took me to the doctor and said the doctor wants to examine me to see if my baby is okay.'

The next day I went to a solicitor, telling them what they had done and asking did they have a right to do it, and my solicitor informed me, because of the case in Scotland, where a child was compos mentis, there was nothing I could do, even though I felt that social services manipulated my daughter to see the doctor.

I rang social services to try and speak with Mrs Wiggins, the social worker, because my daughter did not come home that night. All day I was calling to be told she will return my call. The next day she returned my call.

I asked if she could go and get my daughter from the Salvation Army where Wally was staying. I was informed she doesn't work weekends and I was to ring her on Monday morning to let her know if my daughter had returned home.

I explained that she had already gone into early labor three times and I was worried that she might go into early labor again. Her reply again was "I don't work weekends." She suggested I ring the police and report her missing.

I could not believe what I was hearing about the social worker not caring about my daughter and her unborn child. Nothing I could say to this social worker would persuade her to go and get my daughter away from a dangerous situation. Even when I pleaded with her, she told me to phone the police and report her missing.

That was all I could do. I had a special-needs son at home, and I could not leave him.

I rang the police, explaining the situation, and asked if an officer could go and get my daughter.

The officer told me he had better things to do than dealing with a delinquent teenager. The officer said all I could do was report her missing, but I could not do that until she was missing for 48 hours.

I said to the police officer, 'My daughter was not missing. I know where she is. I just want you to go and get her because I am scared that she might go into premature labor. She had already gone into premature labor three times, and she was with a known drug taker. Could you reconsider because of the circumstances?'

The police officer refused and did nothing and would not go and get my daughter.

All I could do was put the phone down and hope for the best.

All that day I was worried about my daughter, wondering if she had gone into labor or had she taken any drugs. Michelle was easily led.

I rang every maternity hospital I could think of in the area, asking if my daughter had gone into early labor. Thankfully, not one hospital had admitted her. Then I thought, what if she went into labor somewhere in a ditch? I broke down in tears to be interrupted by the telephone ringing.

I picked up the phone and said, 'Is that you, Michelle?'

'No, Mrs Gail, this is the police officer you spoke to the other day, Pc Knob. We have your daughter at the station. We have arrested her boyfriend Wally for possession of drugs.'

I asked the police officer, 'Is my daughter being arrested?'

His reply was, 'No, she is free to go . . . I apologize for not going to the Salvation Army hostel and getting her the other day, but Michelle had insisted I call home, and this is why I am ringing.'

'Thank you for the phone call. I no longer need to worry if my daughter was dead in a ditch. I will arrange for someone to pick my daughter up. Thanks again.'

The arguments continued between my daughter and me, mostly over Wally. She could not see he was no good for her. I tried almost everything to split them up. To my relief, he went into young offenders.

Wally started writing to my daughter. At first, I did not give the letters to my daughter. I wanted to protect my daughter. I even asked the police to intervene because some of the letters were obscene.

I was told by the police I might find them obscene, but my daughter might not, and it was an offence to keep the letters away from my daughter, even though she was under 16 years old. I was told it was her property, not mine.

And a comment was made by the officer. 'She managed to get herself pregnant under the age of 16.'

I felt an awful attitude, when she was still a child. If only social services got my daughter when I asked them, my daughter would not have been pregnant; that, I was sure.

C H A P T E R 3

THE BIRTH OF MY GRANDSON

Wally came out of the young offenders on remand and spent Christmas in my home. I did not want Wally in my home, but my daughter was threatening that she will spend Christmas with Wally, and the only way I knew my daughter would be safe was for Wally to come and stay in my home.

On Christmas Eve, my daughter was complaining of having pains. I called the midwife out, and upon examination, the midwife said my daughter was not in labor. The pain was Braxton Hicks, false labor pains.

All that day the pains were getting worse, and I kept telling my daughter, "You're not in labor. Stop whining."

I was not usually horrible, but my daughter was a baby when it came to pain. But the pains were coming too frequent. In the morning, my daughter did have a little show of blood, but she had a show of blood right through her pregnancy, so I did not take much notice of it. She recently had steroids and injections from the hospital, and she was told it would settle down. The pains were coming every four minutes. Perhaps she was in labor.

I called the hospital and explained that she had six weeks to go to the birth and she just came out of the hospital after having treatment, and I also said that the pain was four minutes apart.

The hospital said, 'Ring an ambulance and get your daughter into the hospital.'

I rang the ambulance, telling them my daughter was in labor.

The operator asked, 'How far apart were the pains?'

I told them, 'Four minutes apart.'

He then said to me, 'Look if you could see the baby's head.'

I told him, 'My daughter has got trousers on.'

'Get them off, and look then.'

I took my daughter's trousers and pants off and looked for the baby's head. I could not see anything, which was good.

I had to wake up my husband to tell him our daughter was in labor, and I called the ambulance, and they were on their way to take me and Michelle to the hospital.

Wally wanted to go to the hospital too. I tried to stop him, but he was creating such a fuss, and Michelle was getting all agitated and saying she was not going to deliver the baby unless Wally was by her side.

I told Michelle, 'If Wally is going, then I am not.'

She said, 'I will have it home then.'

'The baby will die, being six weeks premature,' I said.

A knock came on the door; it was the ambulance. Wally went outside, screaming, 'I will do a car over. You will not stop me from being with the one I love.'

The ambulance men looked at me, wondering what the hell was going on.

I looked back and said, 'Oh, this is Wally, my daughter's boyfriend.'

I had to make a snap decision. I did not want Wally to go to the hospital, and I did not want my daughter to put her unborn child's life in danger. So I knew I had to relent to the idea of Wally going with my daughter and me in the ambulance. I pretended he was not there.

We arrived at the hospital. By this time, the pain my daughter was suffering was so painful. She kept saying to me, 'You promised me, Mum, an epidural. Please, Mum, the pains, help them go away.'

I said to her, 'I will ask the midwife when she comes back into the room for an epidural for you.'

I said to the midwife, 'My daughter is asking for an epidural.'

She said, 'If the womb has not dilated too far, then she can have one. I will have to examine her to see.'

'But you promised me, you promised me,' Michelle said through the pains.

'I know, darling, but you have to be transferred to the delivery suite,' I said.

Michelle gave a slight moan.

The midwife examined my daughter and discovered that her womb had dilated to ten centimeters. It was too late for my daughter to have the epidural I had promised her.

I said to Michelle, 'I did not know you were in labor. Please forgive me.'

I felt so guilty. It was as if I let her down. All I could do was promise to make it up to her later and hope that Michelle will forgive me and realize that I didn't do it deliberately.

In the delivery suite, I had noticed that Wally had stolen needles from the examination room.

I told him that if he did not do as I tell him, then I would get the guards and have him removed. He promised he would do as he was told.

When we first went to the delivery suite, I tried to get Wally out, but the midwife said that it was up to my daughter who she wanted at the birth. Even though I told the midwife he was not the father of my daughter's baby and my daughter was under 16 years old, the midwife still would not listen. I had no choice but to make it as comfortable as I could for my daughter and pretend Wally was not there and only speak to him when I had to.

This is how stupid Wally was—he was sharing the gas and air with my daughter because it made him high. He thought it was funny, but then he would. He was just a kid, just like my daughter was a child.

The labor was very quick and not too painful. Michelle grabbed hold of my hand and bit my hand whilst she was pushing her baby out into the world. Thank heavens, it did not last long. It didn't half hurt.

The staff at the delivery suite was very nice to me, but because my grandson was born premature, he had to be transferred to the intensive-care unit.

The staff at the neonatal unit, at first, was very nice to me too, but then social services got involved, and their attitude changed, and they became disrespectful. Social services had told the staff at the neonatal unit that I had battered my daughter, and the staff talked about me behind my back amongst themselves, and every time I went to see my grandson, snide remarks were made in my presence, like 'That is the woman who battered her daughter,' 'She is going to lose her kids.' The scary stares from the nurses said it all. The look that looked right through you, so spooky. Some of the staff would not say anything to you, but you could guess what they were thinking. Social services also restricted access to my grandson. I made a complaint about the staff on the way I was being treated to the complaints ombudsman, but they did not take it seriously, and nothing was done.

Christmas day came, and my other children opened their presents. It was very strange without my daughter. I did take some of my daughter's Christmas presents in the hospital later that night, and her dad did video her opening her presents, but it was not the same, although the boys did enjoy Christmas.

Without my daughter, it felt like I had a missing child. It was as if she died, although I knew she had not died because she was in the hospital and just gave birth to her child. You never, for one minute, think your child becomes a mum at 15.

When Michelle came home the next day without the baby, I tried to make it Christmas all over again. I had kept some of the boys' Christmas presents behind for them too so they could open their presents with their sister. It was lovely, but it was not Christmas.

At the hospital, I was accused of wanting my grandson for myself because I showed a lot of love to my grandson. I am sure there are lots of grandparents out there who show their love to their grandchildren and they don't get accused for wanting their grandchildren for themselves.

Also, my daughter would not do things for herself like go and get clothes for the baby out of the cupboard by the reception desk. Instead, she would ask me, and I would just do it.

Perhaps this was wrong of me. I just did not mind doing it for my daughter. From an early age, I had always done things for my daughter. I suppose it's seeing my mum do everything for us that I did the same for my daughter. I felt it was my duty as a mum to do things for my children.

When my daughter was younger, she would not speak up for herself. I had to take her to the doctor, and when the doctor asked my daughter what was wrong with her, she refused to answer. And because she was too shy to speak, I would answer for her. I always tried to encourage my daughter to speak up for herself, but she just would not. Then it became a habit, and I spoke for her.

Social services accused me of being too overpowering to my daughter and not allowing her to have her own independence and personality. Yet my daughter was quite able to go and get what she wanted out of life and become an uncontrollable teenager. If what social services said was true, then my daughter would be afraid to say boo to a dickey bird.

I do blame myself for my daughter's rebellious nature, even though I have read many books telling me it was peer pressure that influenced her to take the drugs.

Sadly, my daughter is a victim of rape. I sensed something was troubling her at the time and tried very hard to find out what was wrong. Michelle would not open up and tell me. I did not want to push it because I felt she had a problem with eating, and I took her to my GP

I said to Dr Down Rain that I had concerns that something was troubling my daughter to the extent that she was not eating properly.

His reply was not to worry, it's just her age, all 11-year-olds are finicky with their food, that I should not worry about it.

I don't know why my daughter would not tell me what happened to her, but I do know she told her aunty a year later and begged her aunty not to tell me. She was afraid I would rake it all up by going to the police and having the boy arrested. *Too right, I would!*

All my daughter wanted to do was to try and put it behind her. I know you cannot do this without having some form of counseling. I know this from my own experience. I too was a victim of rape when I was 15. I met a man who was sleeping on my school bus. I too was a rebellious teenager for my mum, but that is another story. All I can say, for many years, it affected me and my relationships. It made me hate sex.

At the age of 11, my granddad molested me, but I was not believed at the time. I took it to my mother, but no one believed me. It was not until my mother was in the hospital, dying, that I asked her, 'Why did you not believe me all those years ago about my granddad molesting me?'

And her reply was, 'It was not that I did not believe you, but he was my father.' She then said, 'If it's any consolation to you, he did it to me and one of your cousins.'

What my granddad did to me affected me for many years, and I never really had a relationship with my granddad because of it, and I hated my grandmother for not stopping it, but I did call him a dirty old man at the time.

My daughter was very promiscuous from an early age. I think it was because of the rape, but only an expert would be able to answer this. My daughter became a victim of rape again at the age of 14, when she was under the influence of drugs. She did take this to me but would not let me do anything about it. She was afraid for her family. The person who raped her told my daughter if she told anyone about it, then her family would be torched alive.

I tried to explain to her that no one has the right to get away with rape and should be punished for a terrible crime.

Michelle said to me, 'The police cannot protect us. You will be torched alive, and even if you go to the police, I will deny that the rape took place, and I will say I was a willing party.'

I was helpless. I could not do anything. I knew my daughter was hurting, but she would not let me go to the police.

CHAPTER 4

CASE CONFERENCE

Two weeks after my daughter gave birth to her baby, social services arranged a case conference. Social services deliberately made it impossible for me to get representation at the case conference, even though they proudly display leaflets in their foyer informing you you are entitled to have a solicitor at a case conference.

It was not until 4:00 p.m. the previous day when we were notified of the case conference. Social services guidelines are that you should be notified five days prior to the case conference. Whether this was done deliberately, I do not know.

My daughter Michelle invited her friend Amy and her dad to the case conference. I was not pleased with my daughter for inviting them as I did not think it would help her case. This is the family my daughter was staying with when she was refusing to come home, when I went to social services begging them to bring her home before she ends up getting pregnant.

My daughter ended up staying with them because I needed a hysterectomy in the hospital and my husband was not able to cope with all the three children at home. My eldest son was under investigation for ADHD. My other boy had learning difficulties. My daughter was difficult to handle; she always seemed to play up against her father. My daughter went to Sea Cadets, and she met Amy there, and her dad was in school with my husband.

I was not happy for my daughter to go and stay with this family because their home was not suitable for my daughter, but I was too ill to argue. I needed this operation because I was anemic and I was having heavy painful periods every two weeks. I needed my life back, and the operation would give me that. It was agreed my daughter would stay there for two weeks, which was how long I would be in hospital.

When I came out of hospital, she was refusing to come home, and I was too ill to argue with her. She stayed with this family for several months. She stayed there because she was given the freedom to do what she wanted. If she wanted to get drunk, she could. If she wanted sex, then she could have sex. If she wanted to take drugs, she could. Not only that, but I also felt the father was too close to my daughter. At one point, I was questioning, was he the father to my grandson?

My daughter knew, if she was home with me, she would have to live by set boundaries, and she had her freedom there. But when she found out she was pregnant, where did she want to go back home?

I was not happy for my daughter to be present at the case conference. I felt that she was too young to understand what was going on around her. It would confuse her so much that she would not be able to explain herself, but social services said they felt she had a lot to offer the case conference. For whom? *Them?* I tried to persuade my daughter not to go to the case conference, but she was adamant she was going.

Before the case conference started, all the professionals were in a small room, discussing my daughter's case. This should never have been allowed. The police officer from the child protection team made a comment to Gail in a teacup. I had noticed the midwife had some kind of report in her hand. The probation officer had one also. I tried to see what report it was. I could not quite see. The midwife and the probation officer put the report down in front of them on the table as they went to sit down.

We were invited to see the chairperson before going into the case conference. My daughter went in and saw the chairperson first on her own. I was concerned that my daughter might have been asked leading questions. I asked her, when she came out, what the chairperson said, and all I got was nothing. I asked her if she understood what the chairperson said to her, and her reply was 'No, not really.' I knew then my daughter was not going to understand what was going to be said in the case conference by her reaction.

It was mine and my husband's turn to meet the chairperson. I was not looking forward to it.

When we went into the room, you could sense the atmosphere. You could tell straight away she did not like me, and she was rather cocky. I could not wait for this meeting to be over. I just stared into space, not listening to what the chairperson was saying.

After a bit, the chairperson said, 'You can go now.'

My mind was somewhere else. I did not realize that she had spoken to me. My husband elbowed me in my waist, and I realized she had been talking to me.

My husband whispered, 'Go.'

'Oh!' I said and walked out of the room.

In the case conference, the tables with chairs in the room were in a neat circle. It reminded me of being back in school.

At the top of the table was the chairwoman, Mrs Hezekiah. Next to the chairperson on her left was her administrator who took the minutes. Left to her were the two police officers from the child protection team. Left to the police officers was Mrs Julian, my daughter's head mistress. To the left of Mrs Julian were my daughter's friend Amy and her dad. Left from Amy's dad was my daughter. Left from my daughter was her dad, and left from him was me. Left from me was the social worker, Mrs Wiggins. Left from her was the health visitor, Mrs Wigg. Left of her was the probation officer, Mrs Founer.

Everyone introduced themselves to one another. For what purpose this was, I don't know.

Apologies were made for the pediatrician for not attending the case conference. His report was there for the chairperson to see. Apologies were also made for my GP.

The chairperson said that the social worker's report had to be shared as there were not enough to go around. Why does that not surprise me?

The report was the same report as the midwife and the probation officer had in the room where they had discussed before coming into the case conference. So that report was obviously what they did not need to share.

The conference started with the social worker's report. It stated that Wally, Michelle's boyfriend, went to the social services department with an accusation that I had physically and emotionally abused her since she was three. My daughter told the social worker that I held her against a wall and beat her up. I then pulled her hair, and whilst Michelle was on the floor, curled up into a ball, I kicked her and punched her until she begged me to stop.

I told the social worker that my daughter exaggerated what had happened. Yes, there was an incident. I did pull my daughter's hair, and I did kick her once, and I do regret doing it.

It was at the time when she was coming down off drugs, when she was being difficult and violent towards me. I had to try and protect myself. I had no help with my daughter, whatsoever. I was the one who got my daughter off the drugs.

Then the social worker read out from a file from previous social work involvement and also added more to the file. I was accused of putting inappropriate footwear that was too tight on my daughter. She also said that my daughter had appointments for her feet.

Social services need to go to Tunisia. They're lucky if they have a pair of shoes, and if they do, they're all holey.

It was wrong information. It was my son who had the appointments for his feet because he was late in walking and they were concerned about him, but the week he had the appointment, my son started to walk.

I always put appropriate shoes on my children because I had a voucher from the government allowing free shoes from Clarks, which measured shoes.

The social worker then said that my daughter was staying out at night and going to nightclubs. That was true when she was staying with her friend Amy, but Amy's dad denied it.

I think, one time, my daughter went to a nightclub when she had a sleepover with her friend in Taffcard, and I got to hear about it from one of her friends in the street. She never got a sleepover again.

The social worker made out that my daughter had gone to nightclubs quite often. Apparently, this is what my daughter told social services. This was obviously wishful thinking on her part.

Then the social services said that, apparently, I went to social services when my daughter was 14, saying that my daughter was taking drugs. The social worker then said it was not the norm for a 14-year-old to take drugs. *You don't say.* And in her professional opinion, it was her home environment that made my daughter take the drugs.

I tried to explain about my daughter's drug use, but the chairperson would not let me explain. She cut me short.

I also tried to explain when the child protection officers came to my home, my house was all upside down. All the wallpaper of the walls were stripped. There were no carpets on the floors. They shouted abuse from the hilltops. I really thought I would be able to redecorate, but I took a job on greater than I could handle because of my illness. Social services should have helped, not criticized. I said to the chairperson that my home had only been like it for a little whilst but nobody believed me.

My daughter had told the social services it was for a long time. I suppose, to her, it was a long time. She told social services she was too ashamed to take any of her friends home. I can understand how she must have felt. I did manage to get the house redecorated, but social services did not try to understand my circumstances: I was separated from my husband at the time because his mother had died, and he was suffering from severe depression, and we were not getting on at the time, and I could not deal with his depression, so I asked him to leave, but he was not taking care of himself, so I said he could come back and I would take care of him but not as a couple.

Social services tried to say that my daughter cared for my special-needs son because I neglected my son. How ridiculous! She could not take care of herself, a special-needs child.

Obviously, this was something my daughter had said to the social worker. My daughter had said that she took care of him because I was mostly in bed all the time.

It was not easy for me to care for my children with the problem I had, and I am not saying my daughter did not help, but she did not care for him on a day-to-day basis.

I could not believe a social worker believed a 15-year-old, a troubled 15-year-old. That was what my daughter was and perhaps still is today. The social worker did not even get her facts right. She said that my daughter was my ex-husband's. That confused my daughter, and she was brought up by her half-brother, and I was married to my son.

Get the names right.

This just goes to show all this social worker did was go into an office, get out a file, and make a report from that. The social worker used the orange book social workers use for a guideline to make accusations.

The social worker also said that I asked for home help because of my husband's depression, when, in fact, it was because I was told I would not be able to lift anything for six weeks, and that is why I was granted home help.

Did it really matter? I needed home help.

After the social worker read her report, the police read theirs. F11s, I think that's what they called them.

The officer said that my daughter had gone missing on numerous occasions and would not say where she had been.

Yes, it is true, my daughter did go missing, and yes, I did call the police because I tried all the obvious places where I might think she might have gone, and it was getting late, and you don't know who is about, and I am a very worrying person like my mum. I was a worry for my mum too. Only, with me, I would run away as a child, but my daughter just stayed out late. But if I knew the police would have put them in an F11s, perhaps I would have thought twice about calling the police to find my daughter.

When my daughter was younger, I strongly believe she suffered from ADD and a defiant disorder but was never ever diagnosed with it. I personally believe she got slipped through the net.

When my daughter went missing, she did not understand that I was worried about her, and every time she went missing, I had to call the police to find her and bring her back. She did not comprehend this and sometimes found it funny.

Even when I told her to stop wasting the police's time and come home on the times she was asked to, she did not comprehend she was doing anything wrong. To her, it was a lovely night, and she was enjoying the night. She did not sense the danger that could have happened to her, and that was like me when I was a child. When I ran away, I never sensed the danger either.

At one time, my daughter went missing, and she fell asleep at a friend's house, and their parents did not know that she was there. The police found her under her friend's bed at 2:00 a.m., and the police brought her home.

Another time, my daughter told her friend she wanted to sleep in her shed. She wanted to find out what it was like to stay out all night, but she knocked the door to come in when she was cold and hungry at three in the morning.

I phoned the police to tell them she was safe, but she refused to say where she was. I discovered a few days later she was only a few doors down the road.

When the game staying out late became not exciting anymore, my daughter did not go out, and the F11s stopped.

After the police report, the midwife read hers. The midwife said I approached her in the supermarket, saying I had concerns for my daughter taking drugs. She felt it was not the appropriate place to tell her and I should have approached her at her office. I could have put it on the supermarket's tannoy.

My daughter had told the midwife I had refused her food and I had often refused her food.

The midwife said, 'She asked for a biscuit, which was on the tray.' They were making a mounting out of a molehill.

My daughter's complexion is very fair, and she is very slim, and on numerous occasions, I have been accused of not feeding my daughter. It is not my fault she has a fair complexion and looks as if she is going to collapse at any moment.

If the midwife had told the full story, then perhaps the professionals in the case conference would not be too quick to judge.

My daughter had just got up, and she had ten minutes to her appointment, and she was having difficulty demanding a cooked breakfast. I told her she did not have time and grabbed a quick sandwich. No, that was not good enough for my daughter. She ran out the street, shouting I had refused her food. She went to the neighbor next door, telling her I refused her food and often refused her food.

The midwife also failed to tell the case conference that her dad took her to a café for a meal after her antenatal checkup.

The health visitor said she had nothing to say as she was just there to represent Dr Heatherup.

The chairperson then asked the social worker if there was anything else she wished to say.

The social worker stood up and said my daughter called into the social services department prior to when I had called into the office and stated my daughter said to the duty social worker she had not eaten all day and said her mother was out, but what my daughter failed to tell the social worker was that she stayed the night with her friend Joy, and she knew I would not be home as I had things to do, and I gave her money for food, but she spent it on sweets and cigarettes.

I did not know at the time my daughter smoked, and I did not know she went to the social services department either. Apparently, when I questioned my daughter about it, she said it was Joy's idea to go there, not hers. Her friend went to the social services department often to get money for food.

The social worker then said the sister of the neonatal unit said that I took over the responsibility from my daughter as if I wanted my grandson for myself. The social worker said I undermined my daughter. She said I was too overpowering for my daughter, and she felt my daughter could not be herself in my presence and said that she felt the baby could not come home from the hospital as the baby would be at risk from me and would be caught up in mine and my daughter's arguments, and she could not guarantee the safety of the child.

I tried to explain to the professionals that I was mature enough not to argue with my daughter, but I could not guarantee my daughter not arguing with me because she is, after all, a 15-and-a-half-year-old child.

I do not want my grandson for myself. I had my children already, and it was my daughter's child, not mine, but bear in mind, she is only a 15-and-a-half-year-old child herself.

My daughter and I talked about where it would be best to put the baby's cot, and we both agreed to put it into my room because her room had severe dampness, and it would make the baby constantly ill, and the baby was premature and vulnerable.

Her room was a box room, and I could not give her the other room because her two brothers were sharing it. Because of my severe asthma, I could not go into the box room myself because of the damp.

I tried to explain these in the case conference, but all the professionals could see is that it was an excuse for me to take over my daughter's duties and be the baby's carer and not my daughter's.

What did it matter who was the carer of the child as long as the baby was getting what it was needed? My daughter would not be able to take care of her baby because of her age and her inability caused by her immaturities. I was prepared to step in, if that is what it took.

I knew my daughter. She was very immature for her age, and it was like a child having a child. But the professionals would not listen. They thought they knew better than me.

The social worker then said my husband suffered from depression, and this would appear to influence our parenting ability.

It seems to me that social workers use this quite often in case conference reports. The social workers will say the parent is suffering from depression, and then they will say you're not a good parent and the children need to be in care.

One in five people will suffer from depression some time in their lives. That is a hell of a lot of children to go into the care system, don't you think?

The social worker, Mrs Wiggins, said I tied my daughter up to a bed when she was two years old.

Yes! This is true. I made a bed harness because my daughter was hyperactive and was getting out of her bed at night and turning the gas fire knobs and the cooker knobs on. There were no safety knob holders when my daughter was young. Thank God for technology, you can get lots of safety things for babies now—cupboard catches, plug safety switches, and lots more—but when my daughter was little, there was nothing on the market.

So I improvised. I made one with baby reins and elastic, but the elastic got caught around her neck, and when she screamed, I realized then what happened. I cut the elastic and never used it again. It was my naivety that made the harness. It was a lesson I learnt, and that is what childrearing is about. There are no books in how to rear your child; it is all experience.

How social services got to know about it? I told my mum. She did not live near me, she was concerned about her grandchild, and she called social services. *Bless her.* I had a social worker for a long time because of my mum ringing up social services. When

I explained what happened, the social worker understood, and no further action was taken. When the social worker had no more concerns, she went away. That is how social services found out it was on file.

The chairperson asked the headmistress of my daughter's school if she would she like to read her report now.

She had said that my daughter had not gone to school for 18 months, and it was sad because she had a lot of potential.

I was not aware my daughter was not going to school other than a few weeks into her pregnancy. I was sending my daughter to school, but she was not going to school. As far as I knew, she was going outside the door to go to school. No one from the school rang me to tell me she was not attending school, and when I asked her about this, she said it was not their responsibility to make sure she was in school but mine.

When I asked my daughter why she did not go to school, she said she was too scared to go to school because she was getting bullied.

I was also told by the education department not to send my daughter to school as the insurance would not cover her because of her pregnancy, but the professionals in the case conference accused me of lying.

Social services also said my daughter was associated with a schedule one offender. Social services accused my husband's friend of being a schedule one offender. When he was told about what was said about him, he got a solicitor involved, and he got a written apology from the head of the social services department, and a lot of staff got transferred to different sections of the department, and some got the sack. But it was said in the case conference, and it looked bad on me. The solicitor for social services told my daughter to get legal representation.

The medical report was read out, and it was said that the marks on her neck were consistent with strangulation marks and the mark on her side consisted of a bruise.

My daughter tried to tell the professionals in the case conference that the marks on her neck were love bites and the bruise on her side was her birthmark. But they would not listen to my daughter or me. In fact, every time my husband or I tried to explain anything in the case conference, the chairperson cut us short and would not let us explain by saying, 'These professionals don't have time to listen to what you have to say.'

I felt that they were throwing accusations at me, at least let me be allowed to defend myself, but I was not given the chance.

The outcome of the case conference was that my daughter was put on the risk register for physical and emotional abuse. My grandson was also put on the risk register for physical and emotional abuse from me, which I found ironic because he was still in hospital.

The chairperson also asked for an investigation, Section 47 under the Children Act, on my two sons.

The social worker recommended to the chairperson that my grandson should not go to my home from the hospital because of the risk from me.

My daughter was advised to go away and consider for her to put her son into voluntary care, bearing in mind if she refused, they would quite easily apply to the courts for a care order, which they would get. So my daughter had no choice but to agree for her son to go into the care system.

The dad of my daughter's friend wrote on a piece of paper ten minutes into the case conference, cut and dried.

Everyone felt they had already made their minds up before they went into the case conference, and all they were doing was going through the motions.

Weeks after the case conference, I telephoned the social services and asked to speak with Mrs Wiggins. I asked if my grandson could home from the hospital and put in all the professional help needed to safeguard my grandson.

The social worker said that it can never be an option to consider for my grandson to come home.

Social services took away the pleasure of her father taking a video of her baby coming out of the hospital. Michelle will never have that memory.

I made a complaint on how the chairperson ran the case conference and the fact that I never had a fair hearing. The complaint was sent to the person I was complaining about.

How can it be independent when it goes to the person you're complaining about?

CHAPTER 5

AT THE HOSPITAL

When my daughter and I visited the hospital to be with her baby, the sister Mrs Bevan's was not very nice to us. In fact, not many mothers liked this sister because of her attitude.

To describe this sister on the ward, one would say she was like a Nazi battle axe, and social services chose this sister to attend a core group meeting, which they had before the case conference without inviting anyone. They did this behind my back.

There was one ward sister whom my daughter and I got on very well with. Why didn't the social services choose that sister, Sister Angel? But no, they had to choose the battle axe because they knew she would provide a bad report on me and on my daughter. This was what they needed to make a case against me for the case conference.

She was the person who said I wanted my grandson for myself. She also said I undermined my daughter and would not let my daughter be herself and took over things from her.

The fact remains—I did it for my daughter because my daughter was lazy, shy, and difficult, and I did not want her to cause a scene, and it was just easier to just go and get them for her.

Most of the nurses at the hospital treated us pretty badly. There was a baby by my grandson whose mother took drugs, and the child was up for an adoption. It was awful for the family. They were treated dreadfully, and I really felt sorry for them, but I did not think I would get the same treatment. I hope no one has to go through what my daughter and I had to go through with the staff in the hospital in the premature baby unit.

My daughter was told that there was a placement for her and her baby at a foster placement but she had to decide there and then. The placement was hundreds of miles away.

I told the social worker she could not make a decision just like that. She needed time to think about it because it would be a big decision. She would be away from her family and her friends. She could not make a decision just like that.

Michelle needed time to think unless it was a ploy to get her away from me and there really was no placement for my daughter. Anyway, she went away to think about it.

The next day Michelle said to me, 'I have to accept the offer social services were offering. I want to be with my son.'

I understood how my daughter felt, being a mum myself.

The next day Michelle and I went down to the social services department and were led to the same room as before.

I thought to myself I would take my bed with me next time as I am a constant user of this room, just changing the wallpaper.

The social worker came into the room, and Michelle said, 'I want to take the offer you offered me yesterday for me to be with my baby.'

Her reply was, 'I cannot offer it to you, Michelle. The offer is not available anymore. It has been taken up by another mum. That is why we told you yesterday you had to agree straight away.'

My daughter started to cry.

I said to the social worker, 'There was not any offer, was there? You just said that because you wanted to put my daughter into the care system and put my daughter's baby up for adoption.'

The social worker's reply was, 'I can assure you, Mrs Gail, there was a placement, but sadly, it has been taken up.'

'You could have held it for a few days. You knew my daughter needed time to think about it. This was not something my daughter could decide there and then, especially the vulnerability of her age. I say to you, there never was a placement.'

I turned to face my daughter and said, 'Come on, let's go home, where we are needed and loved."

It is obvious that Mrs Wiggins, the social worker, needs to go on a course to learn compassion as she obviously lacks in it, and we walked out of the building with our heads held high.

CHAPTER 6

MY GRANDSON'S FOSTER CARERS

I could not believe that social services put my grandson with a foster carer who had nothing—no clothes, no bottles, and not a cot. The foster carer, Sandy Lowen, did not even have a baby bath. She bathed my grandson in a sink, a premature baby with all the germs in the sink. She was not even experienced looking after premature babies, and because of this, my grandson had many chest infections.

Social services asked me for the clothes I bought my daughter for my grandson. At first, I refused on the principle that it was not my daughter's choice for her baby to go into the care system. Then social services were accusing me of depriving my grandson.

I made a list of all the clothes that were given to the foster carer because I did not want any of my grandson's clothes to fall into the care system and go to another child in care as I felt it was the social services' responsibility for another child, not mine.

I was guaranteed, when my grandson grew out of the clothes, I would get them all back, but sadly, many of them went missing, and I was never, ever, compensated for them either.

We had a court hearing at Warry magistrate's court, and it was agreed that my grandson had a guardian ad litem.

I asked my daughter's solicitor about my daughter having a guardian ad litem, but he told me he did not want the courts to see that my daughter was not mature enough to take care of her child.

'But she is only a child herself,' I said.

He ignored me and said he was my daughter's solicitor, not mine.

The magistrates decided that they felt they were not qualified enough, and it was a complex case that they felt needed to be dealt with at the high courts.

Social services decided that they would not pursue the care order on my grandson because my daughter was cooperating with them. It was agreed that she would get five days access to her son at a family center.

I asked at the courts for access to my grandson and my family, but the contact was to be supervised for two hours once a week at the social services department, which meant my two boys only got to see their nephew on school holidays.

I did ask for unsupervised access. There was to be another court hearing.

At that court hearing, it was agreed that my daughter would have an overnight stay at the foster carer's with her son, that will be nice for my daughter, but my access was to stay the same. According to my solicitor at the time, some grandparents don't even get that.

Social services withdrew from asking for a care order because my daughter was cooperating with them. They requested for another hearing.

I was finding access to my grandson very hard because the family carer who was supervising the access, Mrs Duck, was always taking notes. I felt I was being judged with every move I made. I did ask her once why she was taking notes, and she insisted she was just catching up with her work. *Yeah, right.*

She did try to make it comfortable for us and, on many occasions, left us alone for 20 minutes whilst she made coffee. Obviously, she must have felt that I would not harm my grandson in any way. Otherwise, she would not have left me alone with my grandson.

When my grandson was six months old, I requested to take my grandson to go up to a café rather than being stuck in a stuffy room. At first, I was refused, but I kept asking, and when social services could not give any real reason why I could not, I got my wish. I was so glad to show off my beautiful grandson to everyone I knew up town, but I did not know how I was going to introduce the family carer. Do I tell them who she is, or do I pretend I am someone famous and introduce her as my bodyguard? All I can say is to the queen you're welcome to yours ma'am as I do not want another person to follow me ever again in my entire life.

I tried and tried to lose Mrs Dutch, but let's just say she was good at her job. I tried to go into every shop to piss her off, but all she did was smile. Someone must have tried this before. All I wanted was to go shopping on my own with my grandson, like all the other grandmothers do.

After a whilst, I stopped asking to take my grandson up the street as it was not enjoyable anymore. It felt it was not my time with my grandson, and social services changed the family carer, and she was not nice.

My daughter told me that the foster carer was encouraging another foster child to call her mum. I knew the mother of the child and told her what was happening. Because of my actions, social services stopped my daughter's overnight access to her son and cut my access to my grandson one hour for no reason other than saying it is not in the best interest of the child.

I thought this was awfully harsh to do, considering it was I who told the mother, not my daughter. I should have kept my mouth shut. I know this now, but you can't tell someone with Asperger's syndrome a secret because they are not able to keep it.

They moved my grandson to another foster carer who had nothing for the baby again. I could not believe that social services would be so irresponsible to do this to my grandson. They moved my grandson because of what I said and my daughter broke confidentiality by telling me that the foster carer was encouraging her foster child to call her mum. My daughter felt it was wrong, and that is why she told me.

The social services placed my grandson with someone who knew my daughter because her children went to the same school as my daughter, and this should never have been allowed. There in itself was conflict of interest, but no one listened to what I had to say.

There was another court hearing. It was agreed the guardian ad litem would sit in on my access to see if the care I was given to my grandson was in his best interest.

After several sessions of sitting in my contact with my grandson, he recommended the access to be increased back to two hours but not straight away, gradually. I never got my half an hour I was promised, and the guardian ad litem did not care either. Even though it was only a half an hour, every minute spent with my grandson was precious.

CHAPTER 7

MY MOTHER'S DYING WISH

My mum was requesting to see her first great-grandchild. I never told my mum that her great-grandson was in care. I kept coming up with excuses after excuse why my daughter could not come with the baby.

My daughter and I requested the social services and the guardian ad litem for my mum to see her great-grandchild, and it had been agreed in the courts that my mum could see her first great-grandchild. Constantly, we kept asking for my mum to see her great-grandchild. But nothing was being done.

My mum had to go into hospital for a quadruple heart bypass and, sadly, caught the MRSA bug caused by the staff in Wallason Hospital not washing their hands properly in the intensive-care unit.

I said to Mrs Wiggins, the social worker, that I did not think my mum was going to make it. My mum knew that her great-grandson was in the care system by this time because my father had told my mum. I told the social worker it was my mother's dying wish to see her great-grandchild.

The social worker said to me, 'Yeah, yeah, it will be done,' and so did the guardian ad litem said, 'It will be done, Mrs Gail, do not worry.'

Sadly, my mum died before being able to get her dying wish.

A *murderer* on death row gets their dying wish, but my mum was not allowed to have her wish to see her first great-grandchild. That was so devastating. I never thought anyone could be so cruel.

Not only that, but also my mum died before I could say goodbye to her, and it took me a long time to come to terms with it.

I asked the guardian ad litem why my mother never got to see her great-grandchild before she died, and his reply was, 'I thought she had been agreed in the courts. It was up to social services to arrange it. You need to speak with the social services about that.' I agreed to it. And that is all I am saying on the matter.'

The next day I went to social services and asked Mrs Wiggins, 'Why was there no arrangement for my mother to see her great-grandchild? It was granted in the courts, and the guardian ad litem had agreed also. You knew it was my mother's dying wish.'

The social worker's only comment was that she was very sorry but it got caught up in paperwork.

I was so angry with this social worker. I felt inside I wanted to hit her. No one would have blamed me if I had, but I was better than this.

I stood right up to her and screamed into her face, '*Murderers* are given their last rights, but my mother was refused hers. You are a Catholic. How could you do this? May your conscience go with you, and may God forgive you, for I shall not.' I walked past her with my head held high, walking out of the building.

My father got to see my grandson, and it was nice that social services and the guardian ad litem cared enough to take my grandson to see his great-grandfather.

My daughter went to Best Males just after my mum had died for my dad to see my grandson, but I was not allowed to go with my daughter. I did ask, though, but I got refused. It should have not been this way, just my dad getting to see him.

CHAPTER 8

THIS IS WHAT HAPPENED TO MY GRANDSON

My daughter went back to stay with the family where she ended up getting pregnant, and social services encouraged it because they wanted her away from me, and social services were going to allow my grandson to stay with this family. I was so horrified to think that they were going to agree to this, so I complained to the guardian ad litem, saying that it was not suitable for my grandson. The guardian ad litem went and investigated and said that he agreed that it was not in the best interest for my grandson. Whilst my daughter was fighting for her child to be with her, I was fighting for my grandson to live with me, should she lose her case to keep him in the family.

At the same time, there was a case conference on my two boys. From the case conference, it was agreed that there would be two different social workers from a different team to investigate my family home environment.

There was no evidence whatsoever to put my children on the risk register for physical abuse from me. However, there was a pediatrician report saying that he felt that I was suffering from a condition called Munchausen Syndrome by proxy.

I had never heard of this condition whatsoever. It was a severe accusation to put my children on the risk register for emotional abuse from me, and what that doctor had said was a load of bullshit. The doctor said that I deliberately hurt my children to gain attention to myself.

I certainly do not hurt my children to gain attention to myself. If I wanted to gain attention to myself, I would go on *The Jerry Springer Show*.

Because of the pediatrician's accusation, I had to go and see a psychiatrist to be investigated for this condition. I suppose social services had to accuse me of something really serious to get my children on the risk register to say in the courts I was a bad mother and not suitable to take care of my grandson, and this would surely do it.

I went to a psychiatrist, and he was surprised that I was accused of this because he felt that I did not display any of the symptoms. I said to him, 'If I have this condition, then the bloody whole world has it.' I told him that my son had just been diagnosed with ADHD, Asperger's syndrome, and a defiant disorder, and the chartered psychologist felt that I too might have Asperger's syndrome.

His reply was, 'That would explain why they thought you might have Munchausen syndrome by proxy because you would sometimes come over aggressive and threatening.'

I tried to tell social services in the beginning that my son was under investigation for ADHD, but they did not believe me. They felt my children's behavior was because they were being abused as the behavior traits were very similar to that of an abused child, and the social workers were not trained to recognize the traits of a child with autistic disorders. Social services were not interested in my eldest boy because he was old enough to tell them "to get lost, I am going to live with my parents," but my other boy could not talk because he had special needs. I was sure they had thought I had caused his disabilities by physically and emotionally abusing him.

I asked a psychologist when she came to my house, in her professional opinion, was it possible for abuse to make a child handicapped, and she told me no, the child would recover when the child was out of the environment; whereas, a child with learning difficulties would not.

It really affected me to think that the social services thought I could do that to my son. I love my boy, and I am a good mum and certainly would not hurt him in any way.

It was decided that my daughter was to be given a chance for her to care for her child at a mother-and-baby unit.

My husband and I helped to settle her in. I gave everything that I bought for my grandson, like the cot, carry cot, bottles, sterilizer, blankets, sheets, and clothes. She seemed to be happy, and I worried about whether she would be able to cope on her own with no help from anyone.

My grandson was not going there until the next day as social services felt my daughter needed time to settle in.

My daughter's room was very nice. It consisted of a single bed, a wardrobe, and two chest draws, all made of teak wood.

My daughter went out the day before with the social worker and bought a pillow, duvet, and duvet cover for her bed, which was moon and stars. It looked very nice and had a very calming effect.

The staff at the mother-and-baby unit was very nice to me, at first, until the next day. I was refused to see my daughter, and when I asked why I was refused, I was told that social services said I could only go there for my access and they were only carrying out their orders and if I did not like it, take it up with the social worker.

The manager of the mother-and-baby unit slammed the door in my face. *How rude!*

The next day I rang social services and asked why I was refused to see my daughter.

She told me that my daughter was being monitored on how she can cope with the baby and she was on a three-month trial, and if she coped very well, then she would go into a house in the front on her own with the baby. Then I would be able to see her.

I asked what kind of support my daughter will be getting with my grandson as I am not allowed to help in any way. I said to the social worker that I felt my daughter was so young. Without practical help, my daughter was sure to fail.

I was told to mind my own business and it was up to her and her manager to decide if any support would be given to my daughter and I was to keep my nose out where it was not wanted.

I knew then that social services were setting my daughter up to fail. There was nothing I could do to help my daughter.

My grandson was a colicky baby, and he did not sleep much during the day or night. My daughter needed a lot of help, and all she got was monitoring instead of practical help.

I tried to tell them that my daughter was unable to cope because of her immaturity, but no one would listen to me. She was 16, for god's sake.

I got married at 16 and had my son at 18, and I was not mature then, and my son went to my parents because I was not mature enough to take care of him, and I was 20. It was like history repeating itself.

Social services also changed the venue for my contact to my grandson. I could not observe how my daughter was doing. There was nothing I could do. My hands were tied.

I rang my daughter to see how she was coping, but social services would complain and say I was keeping her away from taking care of my grandson and I upset her every time I rang.

It was not true. I did not upset her. There was always someone listening to mine and my daughter's conversation. We could not have a private conversation.

Two social workers came to my home to investigate how I was caring for my two boys. After coming for a few months, they said to me, 'We are not seeing what the other social workers said about you, Mrs Gail. We can see that you really care for your children and take care of them very well. We are happy with what we see, and we shall be making a report to say this.'

I then asked, 'Could you make a report for the courts to say that I would take great care of my grandson as well?'

'We are not able to do that, sorry, it is not our case, and we cannot step on anyone else's toes.'

It is ironic I told social services that they got it all wrong with me but no one was listening.

The social worker, Mrs Wiggins, had taken it personally with me. She was not doing her job properly. She was letting her feelings interfere with her professionalism, but there was nothing I could do and no one I could go to to get them to realize the social services were making a big mistake.

It was ordered at the courts that Mack Awarter, the guardian ad litem, will do a report to see if my grandson would be able to live with his grandparents, should my daughter fail to get her son back. It was also ordered that a psychologist would do a report on me and my family.

Wally had been released from young offenders, and he was allowed to visit my daughter at the mother-and-baby unit, even though my daughter told the social worker she did not really want to see him.

The staff at the mother-and-baby unit did not want any trouble from him, and they thought, once he had seen my daughter, he would be on his way, but it did not happen that way. Instead, my daughter saw him several times.

The social worker had plans for him to share in the care of my grandson. I could not believe that they were willing to allow a known drug user, with a conviction with GBH, to care for my grandson, and they were saying I made bad judgements concerning my daughter.

I told the guardian ad litem the intentions of the social services. He went absolutely livid, and social services were accusing me for being a bad mother *what a cheek!*

I went to my access for my grandson, and the coordinator, Mrs Hamsouth, had every opportunity to have called me into a room and told me that social services were taking our grandson back into the care system. I could have prepared my daughter for the devastating news, but no, Mrs Hamsouth had to come into my access, telling my daughter, knowing how much it would hurt my daughter and spoiling my contact with my grandson.

My daughter reacted adversatively towards me, and this is what social services wanted. They wanted to be able to say to the courts that our relationship was volatile.

It was just a teenager reacting to bad news. How the hell did they expect her to behave when they took her child away?

Mrs Hamsouth told my daughter that the staff at the mother-and-baby unit told social services that my grandson's safety could not be guaranteed against my daughter. So what I said to Mrs Wiggins about my daughter not being able to cope without practical help was, in fact, true. If only someone would have taken notice of what I was telling them about my daughter, but no one would listen.

My daughter was told she could not go back to the mother-and-baby unit and she had to agree for her baby to go back into the care system.

I was told that the mother-and-baby unit had been robbed, and they suspected Wally to have robbed the mother-and-baby unit, and I think this had an influence on the decision to get my daughter out of the mother-and-baby unit, but it took Mrs Hamsouth great pleasure telling my daughter that she could not go back to the unit. This woman was a very cruel woman, and she was a social worker before.

God help the mothers who have to use the family center.

All social services had to do was to say to a judge *there is a likelihood of harm*.

I personally feel that this in itself needs to be changed in the Children Act. A proof there is harm should be shown because a lot of children are wrongly going into the care system because of this statement.

The staff at the mother-and-baby unit refused me or my daughter to go and pack her belongings.

I could not believe that the unit was run by a Christian organization, and this is how they treated my daughter: They dumped all her belongings into black rubbish bags outside the mother-and-baby unit, and stuff got broken, and not only that, but they also kept my grandson's clothes. I demanded them back because they were not the property of the social services.

When my daughter got kicked out of the unit, social services offered to pay half of a bed and breakfast because she was refusing to come home. She went back to the family where she ended up getting pregnant.

When my daughter had five-day access to her child, she was not entitled to any benefits because she was not in school or college.

Social services expected me to support my daughter, even though she was not living at home.

I did what I could but, it was never enough for social services. I told the guardian ad litem that I had my suspicions that I felt that the father of my daughter's friend was the father of my grandson, but he did not believe me. He accused me of causing problems within their family.

I asked if they could do a DNA test because he had a rare blood group, but it was ignored. If only I could find out what my grandson's blood group was, then I would know for sure. I was told I had no proof and the test cost too much money. Maybe social services already knew.

Christmas time came round again, and my grandson was one, and my daughter did want to come home for Christmas, but she came later on that night to show a video that was taken that day.

On the video, she had been drinking, and she was somewhat drunk, and she said to her friend Amy, 'Does my bum look big in this?'

Amy's dad was taking the video of her and said, 'Oh yes,' and he was taking a video of not only her bum but also of her breasts, and you could hear slight moans on the video as if he was being turned on.

All it did was to make me believe even more that he was the father of my grandson.

My daughter was so angry with the social worker for taking her baby away, and she went to see her social worker, and she lost her temper with her and pinned her against the wall and slapped the social worker in the face. My daughter did what I wanted to do. Because of what my daughter did, they took the social worker off the case and appointed another social worker.

Mrs Wiggins did not prosecute my daughter, but she did ask for an apology from my daughter.

Yes, they gave my daughter a lovely social worker.

Yes, you guessed it.

Mrs Hamsouth, the family coordinator, a nice lady. (I think not.)

My daughter had to go to her solicitor, and I had to go to mine to get access to my daughter's son. My daughter fell out with her friend, and she came back home to live. She did not have a bed, she slept on the couch, so it was only a matter of time for her to want to come home.

There was a court hearing where I applied for leave to the courts for a residency order for my grandson to live with me.

Judge Gasket felt I did have merit to apply for leave, but social services thought I would not get leave from the courts. This was the beginning of the fight.

God was on my side that day, and the judge valued law and order and remembered why he became a judge in the first place. Had I not gotten it, I would have had to appeal against the decision, and it would have taken a long time, and my grandson would have surely gone for adoption at that time.

Miss Myron, a psychologist, wrote a report about high warmth and low criticism, and the guardian ad litem felt that Mrs Hovell would be appropriate to do a report on relationships within the family. Apparently, this psychologist worked with this lady. I had no objection to her doing her report. It was a long time before she came to my house to do her report, and I was concerned that she would not do it in time. Eventually, she came to my house, and I was not there. I was out shopping, and it pissed her off. She came back to see me. She asked lots of questions about my daughter and how I felt my daughter would cope, and I told her the truth that I did not think that she would be able to cope unless she got lots of help. I told her that I felt, as a child, she probably had ADD with a defiant disorder but got slipped through the net.

She never asked any questions about parenting or about relationships within the family. All she seemed to do was fill out forms about ADHD. She said she was coming back to see me as she had many more questions to ask, but she never came back.

The guardian ad litem had to do his report too. He came to see me and my family. I sensed he did not want to be in my home, and he was just going with the motions. It felt as if he was not on my side, but apparently, my solicitor said it is very rare for the guardian ad litem to be in favor for the grandparents.

My opinion, a guardian ad litem is nothing more than a lapping poodle for social services.

When the psychologist came to my house, she talked to a budgie made out of mushrooms. This lady really thought it was real. You might ask why anyone would have a bird made out of mushrooms in a birdcage. My bird had died, and I saw this imitation bird in a jewelry store, and I thought it would look nice in a birdcage. I gave Mr Water, the guardian ad litem some juice, but he knocked it over on my lovely carpet.

Just don't invite him to your parties.

I know that the guardian ad litem felt that I suffered from Munchausen syndrome by proxy because he was a psychiatric nurse before he was a guardian ad litem.

Shame on you, Mr Water.

Never mind, there are many innocent bystanders in this world who will be accused of this fictitious illness.

The dreaded court hearing came and lasted five days. In the courtroom, there was like a pulpit, where a judge was sitting high, looking down on his subjects. There was a table and a chair with a funny-looking machine, like an adding machine, where a lady was typing away, probably doing the minutes of the court hearing. To the right was another looking pulpit, where you had to stand and swear with a Bible in your hand and swear to tell the truth, the whole truth, and nothing but the truth. There was a long table where all the barristers and solicitors sat, and then there were chairs all around the room for other people to sit. The room had an atmosphere you could not say what you wanted to. It felt dark and dreary as if the devil were in the room. The judge just wore a black gown without a wig as well as the barristers. The solicitors wore suits.

It was time for me to be cross-examined by the social services barrister. He was very hard on me. It was like he took a personal dislike and wanted to make me cry, which he did. I wonder if there was a conscience in his brain. I think the barrister had been at his job too long.

The judge told me I was not to talk to anyone as I was still given evidence. To be honest with you, I was too tired to talk with anyone.

The second round of questioning was not so bad. Perhaps he was thinking of his holidays as he was going on holiday abroad.

My daughter's barrister asked me questions. He was quite nice.

The guardian ad litem barrister, she was not so forceful. I think she could see that I was unfairly treated by the social services barrister, so she tried to be kind.

My daughter was next in the dreaded witness box. They treated my daughter with kindness probably because they knew she was only 16 years old.

I had a report from the chartered psychologist, telling the judge about my son's condition, but Judge Masters would not accept the report. He said he would read the report but will put the evidence as background evidence, but they did accept a report on the day of a hearing from the social services department. The judge would not accept the report because he would have had to accept my children's behavior was caused by their disabilities and not because of my parenting skills.

The guardian ad litem gave his evidence in favor of the social services.

The psychologist gave her evidence. She felt that I was not consistent with the discipline I gave with my son and I did not know how to say no to him. This was very interesting because she had only seen me and my son once together for three minutes. How could she make this observation in three minutes? For her to be able to come to this conclusion, she would have to have been a genius, and this is the psychologist who talks to birds made out of mushrooms, and so dithery, she forgets to turn off her mobile phone in the courts.

My barrister asked why she did not go back to me to ask those vital questions. Her reply was she felt she did not need to. If that is how she does her report, *God help the people who employ her.*

I was criticized for taking my son to the courts, but I could not leave him on his own because he has learning difficulties.

Social services and the courts knew my son had an inset day, but they were not prepared to change the day for my husband's evidence, and not only that, but social services also never offered any help for someone to look after him.

I also found out that the psychologist was best friends with the guardian ad litem.

When the social services first came into my family, my house had bare walls with no wallpaper and no carpets other than mats all over the place, and there were black bags all over the house, which they thought was dirty washing but, in fact, was clean washing. I had just had a hysterectomy, and I was not well enough to do anything.

Yes, if I went into someone's house looking like that, I would question what the hell was going on, but I would have helped and not criticized.

All social services did was shout abuse from the rooftop instead of looking at the dynamics of the problem and saying to themselves, as good social workers, how we can help this family and not try to destroy this family.

My daughter's barrister then said that she was not given a chance to prove to be a mother and quoted lots of law and talked about a case which was beyond my understanding.

Then my barrister said his piece, saying that if my daughter failed to gain custody, then I would want to be looked at for a residency order.

The guardian ad litem barrister did his summoning up, saying my boys were on the risk register for emotional abuse, and because they were on the risk register, it was a cause of concern.

Social services were keeping my children on the risk register deliberately for their benefit to say to the courts they were on the risk register.

My daughter stayed with me whilst the court hearing was going on. She had her own home. By this time, the council gave her a three-bedroom house, but she did not want to be on her own.

Whilst at the courts, my daughter got burgled. She had jewelry stolen. The jewelry was what I had given her and bought for birthdays and Christmas. Also, CDs were stolen. In fact, what the burglar did was take her sheet off her bed and put all the things in the sheet to steal.

She had some idea of who it might have been. She told the police who it was, but they really did not care and did nothing to catch him. It was awful for her.

The burglar even stole her underwear, and it looked like the burglar stayed in her house for days and ate her food and brought a dog with him.

The police came and took fingerprints, but they said there was no sign of forced entry. Sadly, she could not shut her windows properly because they were broken and she was waiting for them to be fixed.

This was all she needed. She was trying to fight in the courts for her son and have this happening.

It did turn out to be the person she thought it was. She found out months later, when she talked with him, he had been on drugs.

My barrister, summing up, said to the courts that I would never be able to take care of any of my grandchildren at any time. I went to stand up and ask my barrister who's side he was on, but my solicitor told me to sit down because I will be in contempt of court. I could not believe my barrister was saying this to the courts. He had been bribed or something. There was no way he could say that to the courts because each situation has their own circumstances.

It was agreed that they were going to try my daughter with her brother up in Mouthbourne, and the baby would be slowly introduced to her in several months, and my access would be fizzled out when the baby is up with his mother.

My eldest boy my mum brought up was in the area selling flowers for charity. He found out from my mum when she was in the hospital that his sister's baby was in the care system, and he wanted to help his sister. He lived in Mouthbourne, and he was offering for his sister to live with him and his girlfriend, and he would foster his sister and his nephew.

In theory, this was wonderful for my son to offer his help for his sister, but in practice, it was diabolical. I knew that my son was taking drugs, and I knew my daughter. She would not heed to boundaries.

I could not see this ever happening because of the fears what I knew to be true, and I told social services this and the guardian ad litem that it would not work, but they would not listen to what I had to say. All they thought was I was after my grandson for myself, when, in reality, I knew my daughter, and I knew my son was taking drugs and his relationship with his girlfriend was rocky.

It was not that I did not want my daughter to have her child, I just knew she was not mature enough to take care of her baby, and if my son was not on drugs at the time, I would have not had any reservation with him fostering his sister or my grandson. I just could not sit back and let my grandson go into that environment.

My daughter went to Mouthbourne to be with her brother, but it never worked out up there. She would not listen to her brother and stayed out all hours, and she got involved with her brother's friend who also took drugs and ended up getting pregnant, and the pressures my daughter put onto my son split up their relationship, and my grandson never ever went to be with his mum.

Social services told my daughter she will not be able to take care of two children. She had to decide which child she wanted to keep, but she could not keep them both. So she decided to keep the child she was carrying because she felt she had more of a chance of keeping her baby than she would with the other child. Social services already had the care order because my daughter signed the care order. My daughter had to agree to an adoption order in order for her to keep her child she was keeping.

I was told my solicitor that I did not stand a hope in hell of a chance to fight for my grandson. So I had no option but to let him go.

You cannot win the government. They have the courts in their pockets, the guardian ad litem on their side, and the money to pay for the best barristers and solicitors in the world.

But I gave them the fight as good as I could.

My conscience is clear.

I am the best mum there is.

Yes, I made mistakes with my daughter, but I am only human.

I only wish I could have fought it further.

But you can't win the government.

* * *

Update: My grandson had been in the care system for 18 years and was adopted by the foster carer when he was 18. He searched out his mother, and then he searched me out. He has a very good relationship with his mother, although he does not call her mum, and he calls me by my name, but that's okay. He knows I have always loved him and will continue to love him and be there for him. He has his own place, so he is independent. He can call on me anytime he likes. I have helped him financially because he is unemployed, and this is what nanas do. He says his childhood was very happy, and I am pleased the foster carer loved my grandson as her own. So it is not all too bad. We will continue with our relationship. I speak with him frequently on Messenger. He took his adoptive grandfather's name, which is the same surname as my mum's. She will be happy up in heaven.

I only wish my son my parents brought up would forgive me for abandoning him when he was 18 months old. I know he knows I have always loved him and will always love him until the day I die, but he doesn't want a relationship with me because he said he feels nothing for me. That hurts, but there is nothing I can do but love him. Hopefully, he will deal with his demons and contact me for a lovely relationship because I am a nice person.